I Am that I Am

BEVERLY D. KENNARD

BALBOA.
PRESS

A DIVISION OF HAY HOUSE

Balboa Press books may be ordered through booksellers or by contacting:

Balboa Press
A Division of Hay House
1663 Liberty Drive
Bloomington, IN 47403
www.balboapress.com
1 (877) 407-4847

Because of the dynamic nature of the Internet, any web addresses or links contained in this book may have changed since publication and may no longer be valid. The views expressed in this work are solely those of the author and do not necessarily reflect the views of the publisher, and the publisher hereby disclaims any responsibility for them.

The author of this book does not dispense medical advice or prescribe the use of any technique as a form of treatment for physical, emotional, or medical problems without the advice of a physician, either directly or indirectly. The intent of the author is only to offer information of a general nature to help you in your quest for emotional and spiritual well-being. In the event you use any of the information in this book for yourself, which is your constitutional right, the author and the publisher assume no responsibility for your actions.

Any people depicted in stock imagery provided by Thinkstock are models, and such images are being used for illustrative purposes only. Certain stock imagery © Thinkstock.

Print information available on the last page.

ISBN: 978-1-5043-7316-6 (sc)
ISBN: 978-1-5043-7317-3 (hc)
ISBN: 978-1-5043-7318-0 (e)

Library of Congress Control Number: 2017900499

Balboa Press rev. date: 01/31/2017

INTRODUCTION

Our great, awesome, "I AM" is truly a "Living God". He is not a God made with human hands. We didn't create Him, He created us in His image. My main reason for writing this book is that the Lord wanted me to write it! He wants to show others how much He loves them by the way He blessed me in little ways and big ways. I think that it's the little blessings that show His greatest love.

I see too many Christians who don't appear to really believe that God will answer their prayers. I don't understand why, if they don't believe this, that they take on His name? I came to a point in my life where I had to know whether He was real or not. Was He truly the God described in the Bible? If not, then there was no point in putting my faith in Him. As I cried out to Him with all of my heart, the great "I AM" proved to me that He is not only as the Bible portrays Him, but more. The Bible says, "And you shall seek me, and find me, when you search for me with all your heart". (Jeremiah 29:13)

At this point in the history of our world, I believe we are truly in the last days. Evil abounds more and more. It is crucial that Christians develop a true relationship with the "Only true God". We need His strength, wisdom, love, protection; in short, we need the reality of our living God (Jesus) in our lives in order to survive the coming persecution. I pray that all who read this book will be encouraged to reach out to our awesome, loving and forgiving God and experience His embrace. He is the 'MOST HIGH" and it is of the UTMOST importance that we recognize Him as such and give Him the respect and love He deserves. When we do this, He responds in manifold blessings far above and beyond what we give Him. To spend five minutes in the Lord's presence is worth more than an eternity with all the riches this world has to offer! As you read this book where I share some of my experiences with our great "I AM", I pray that the Holy Spirit will reveal Himself to you in a special way.

NOTE: All Scripture quotations are from the AUTHORIZED VERSION Commonly called the King James Bible.

CHAPTER I

This is the name God gave to Moses when Moses asked, "Who shall I tell them sent me", Exodus 3:13 &14. [13] And Moses said unto God, Behold, when I come unto the children of Israel, and shall say unto them, The God of your fathers hath sent me unto you; and they shall say to me, What is His name? What shall I say unto them?

[14] And God said unto Moses, I AM THAT I AM: and He said, Thus shalt thou say unto the children of Israel, I AM hath sent me unto you.

I understand this to mean, whatever you need me to be, **I AM**. Also, from God's perspective, whatever He needs to be to accomplish his work, He is. He is totally self sufficient. He does not need anyone or anything. He chooses to work through us, because He loves us and it results in blessings for us when He uses us.

This does not mean that He needs us in order to do His work. He does "delight" in us, His creation. Proverbs **8**:[30] Then I was by Him, as one brought up with Him: and I was daily His delight, rejoicing always before Him;

It gives me a tremendous feeling of security and peace knowing that my God is able to take care of anything that comes against me. Isaiah 43:11 states, "I, even I, am the LORD; and beside me there is no saviour." Isaiah 9:6 states, "For unto us a child is born, unto us a son is given: and the government shall be upon His shoulder: and His name shall be called Wonderful; Counselor; The Mighty God; The Everlasting Father; The Prince of Peace."

This seems obvious to me that it is referring to our Lord and Saviour, Jesus Christ.

During the past thirty-six (36) years the Lord has revealed Himself in my life in many different ways. I have felt the Lord encouraging me to share much of what He has been and done for me so that others will know that He is still alive and well and continues to work in our lives as He did in the days of the early church.

All we need to do is to BELIEVE that He is real and He will answer us when we call.

As stated in Malachi 3:6 "For I am the LORD, I change not:", and Hebrews 13:8 "Jesus Christ the same yesterday, today, and for ever." This book is a part of the "dream" or vision, whichever you choose to call it, that He; the **Great I AM** has given me.

Psalm.66:8 "O bless our God, ye people, and make the voice of His praise to be heard."

It is my prayer that my voice of His praise will encourage others to believe in our **Great I AM**

I have been a believer in God the Father, Son and the Holy Ghost, who are one, for as long as I can remember. My parents believed and told us that God created the heavens and the earth, but didn't really talk about their faith much. My mother did have several warnings of impending danger and because of one of these warnings, one of my brother's life was spared. She also had a personal spiritual deliverance from a deep depression which she was unable to pull herself out of. At the point of suicide she called out to Jesus and He delivered her. As I remember her telling me about it, when she went to bed she told the Lord that if He didn't help her, she feared that she would commit suicide. Suddenly she was aware of someone lifting her out of her bed and carrying her down a long hallway. There were closed doors on either side except for one door which was open slightly and a tiny bit of light shone out into the hallway. The person carried her into that room which had a long table in the center. He laid her on the table then left the room. She said there was just a tiny light in one corner in the ceiling and somehow she knew she had to keep her eyes on that light and that she would be safe.

Then she felt a whirling sensation in her chest. It began as a small circle and kept growing larger and faster. As the sensation increased so did the Light in the room. She said it continued until she felt as if her chest was about to explode and then it stopped and the room was full of Light. The person who brought her here returned; carried her back to her bed and left. She said the room was still full of Light and she thought she must have left her reading light on but as she reached up to turn off the light the room was dark. The depression was gone. She said she had never felt so happy in her life as she did at that moment and the joy continued into the next day.

When she awoke in the morning she still had that overwhelming joy and peace. The depression was gone and did not return! Praise Jesus! (John 6:8 Jesus said : I am the LIGHT of the world.)

I learned the basic Gospel at our local church, but somehow no one ever told me you had to invite Jesus into your heart and accept him as Lord of your life. This was explained to me by a Baptist gentleman who worked with a man I was currently living with. One day I saw this gentleman reading his Bible and I asked what he was reading. The end result of that conversation was that I accepted Christ not only as LORD, but as LORD of my life and invited Him into my heart. It was a very special moment for me and I cried. This took place in the summer of 1974.

I developed a hunger to know more about the Lord and wanted to get to know Him on a personal level. Within a month or two after I had acknowledged Jesus as LORD and invited Him into my heart to be LORD of my life, He revealed himself as my leader when He led me to a Spirit filled church. By this I mean a church that believes in the baptism of the Holy Ghost whereby the gifts are made manifest for believers today.

For the first time in my life I saw people doing what the Bible says believers should do.

(Mark 16: [**17**] And these signs shall follow them that believe; In my name shall they cast out devils; they shall speak with new tongues; [**18**] They shall take up serpents; and if they drink any deadly thing, it shall not hurt them; they shall lay hands on the sick, and they shall recover.

I saw people being healed after they were anointed with oil and the pastor and others layed hands on them and prayed. They also spoke in tongues "As the Spirit gave them utterance". (Acts 2:4)

Years later I would see visions; experience dreams wherein the Lord spoke to me and the working of miracles besides being healed of ovarian cancer.

After leading us to the Spirit filled church, He convicted me of the sin in my life. I was living with a man outside of wedlock.

Psalm 23:3 states, "He leads me in the paths of

righteousness for His name's sake." When we become born again (definition of a Christian), we are taking on his name and He expects us to walk uprightly before Him. Does this mean we live without sin? No, that is an impossibility. As long as we live in this human body we still have the sin nature. However, we also have the Holy Spirit within us to help us resist temptations. (Romans 7 :20-25)

I Peter 1:16 states, "Be ye holy; for I am Holy."

The Holy Spirit was working on my conscience but I did not pay attention. I continued to live in sin. Then one day we went to visit one of my brothers and his wife. As we were walking up the walk way to their home, my brother came out to meet us. He told us that we could not come in because his wife said as long as we were living together, she could not let us in her home. He apologized but said, "she says that is what the Bible says we are supposed to do and I have to respect her wishes."

I Corinthians 5:11 states, "But now I have written unto you not to keep company, if any man that is called a brother be a fornicator, or covetous, or an idolater, or a railer, or a drunkard, or an extortioner; with such an one no not to eat."

Now I realize a lot of people will take issue with this and say it's too extreme. However, this was her understanding at the time and she stood up for her convictions. I admired her for that. It was one of those moments when you wish the ground would open up and swallow you and it really hurt deeply. In spite of the hurt, I knew she was right and what I was doing was wrong. In this moment our Lord revealed Himself as Chastiser.

Hebrews 12:6 "For whom the Lord loveth He chasteneth, and scourgeth every son whom He receiveth."

Our loving Father had convicted me of this sin and gave me ample time to correct the situation before He used my brother and his wife to chastise me. This event was followed a little while later with a visit to my pastor. I wanted to talk to him about problems I was having in my relationship with the man I was living with. My pastor very bluntly said, "Well Bev, how can you expect our Lord to work in your life when you know you are living a life that is not pleasing to Him?"

Finally, I decided that I could not continue in this lifestyle. The Holy Spirit was working on my conscience so greatly that I just simply could not take any more. I told the man (let's call him Peter) that we had to stop living in sin and either get married or live separately. We were married about one month later. This would prove to be a mistake. The marriage ended in divorce ten (10) years later. Being a "babe in Christ" which means, a new Christian, I didn't know that I could ask the Lord about such things and expect an answer. It just seemed logical to me that 'He would want us to get married and Peter was wiling to do so. It takes time to learn to hear the Lord's voice. Jesus said in John 10:27 "My sheep hear my voice, and I know them, and they follow me." The problem is that we don't recognize the voice we hear as His at first. We think it's just our own thoughts. In time we learn to recognize it. It is also especially difficult to hear Him when our emotions are involved. Most of the time we just want Him to go along with what we want.

In I Chronicles 28:9 King David told his son Solomon to "serve the LORD with a perfect heart and with a willing mind."

Often our hearts are in the right place but our minds aren't in syncronization.

King David also said in this Scripture, "If you seek Him, He will be found of thee."

This proved to be very true for me.

It was at this church where we met and became friends with the associate pastor and his wife. It was he who performed the marriage ceremony for us. They continued to be my friends for years. The Lord also gave him a ministry.

CHAPTER 2

MY TEACHER/PROVIDER

Shortly after we were married the Lord led us to Christian Full Gospel meetings. My husband seemed to enjoy these and I also enjoyed them. They were very informative and we received some ministry from them. It was at one of these meetings that I heard of another Christian group for women only. I began to attend these meetings and the Lord blessed me tremendously. I received much encouragement and "hands on" prayer plus instruction for my daily walk in Christ Jesus. Attending these meetings helped me to "fit in" with other Christians. I found out that I wasn't the only one with left over baggage from life outside of Christ. These women came from all walks of life and were very kind and compassionate. They did not judge me or condemn me for the life I led before.

It was here that I met a very special lady who would become a wonderful friend. This lady took me under her wing and often would tell me of special retreats or conventions for women. If I was interested, she would pay my way to attend. One time she made a coat for me. I was searching for employment and the only coat I had was old and quite worn. She came to me and said, "I know you are looking for employment and you could use a new coat so, I thought I would help you out as much as I can. If you will allow me to, I would be happy to make a coat for you."" Can you imagine? I never refused clothing, especially new. She had a husband and three children of her own so she couldn't afford to buy one for me but she did have some extra material which she made into a beautiful coat. It was a long one with a tie belt. I loved it! She also invited my husband and I for numerous dinners, knowing that we could not return the favor. This is the true Christian way. Her presence in my life was ordained by Jesus. Through the years the Lord has used her to send a word of encouragement and wisdom wherever I was at exactly the right time. She always knew when I was having problems and was quick to call. During this time Jesus was revealing Himself to me through His Word and through the people He brought into my life as a kind and loving Savior and provider.

CHAPTER 3

Up to this point, the Lord has been "my Redeemer/ Savior, Leader, Provider, Chastiser, the Righteous One, Teacher and Encourager. He will continue to be all of these throughout my life in addition to other things.

Peter was a musician and was quite accomplished at his trade. When we first met, he was a school teacher only playing in a band on the weekends. His teaching career came to an end during the first year we were together and my life with him changed from that point on. He asked me if I would be willing to try to play bass guitar, and I said yes. It seemed that I was kind of a natural at it and really enjoyed it. As he set his heart and mind on earning a living through music, mine were more interested in getting to know Jesus better. This sounds very pious on my part but it honestly is true. Soon, we had sold our home and were traveling across country.

The Lord continued to bless me and lead us to excellent churches. He also revealed himself as my protector while driving vehicles across the country that were not in very good condition. One time a tire almost came off while I was driving. The gas pedal suddenly went to the floor with no resistance and without any response from the truck. I told my husband something was wrong and when I explained, he told me to not touch the break and to pull over to the breakdown lane as gently as I could. I did as he instructed me and when we finally came to a stop we discovered that all the nuts that hold the tire on had sheared off. The truck had wide rims so the tire stayed on but it was right on the edge of the rim. Our Lord was definitely watching over us. This was on a major highway out in one of the western states. Wide open country with not much civilization around. There was one farm house about a mile away and my husband was able to get the parts he needed; but he had to fix it himself. Jesus promises to be our shield and buckler which means a protector. Some people will say these things are just coincidence, but I believe that once we become a child of God, He watches over us and protects us much more than we realize.

On one other occasion we were traveling from TN to NH and one tire was so worn the cords were showing. My husband told me to pray for a garage where we could at least buy a spare. It happened to be a Sunday so all the garages were closed, but

suddenly he spotted one that appeared to be open.
The owner was just locking the door as we drove up.
When my husband explained our situation he said,
"Well I have a pile of tires out back. Go take a look
and if you find something you can use, take it." We
found a tire close enough to the size of our other tires
so that we could use it as a spare. It was mounted
on a rim and inflated. Ready to go. We did not need
to use it though; we got all the way to northern NH
on well worn tires. Praise the Lord!

CHAPTER 4

MY DELIVERER AND MY STRENGTH

In Jan. 1980 my husband was really on my case to quit smoking. I knew he was right in this matter. Smoking is bad for our health. It is also very unpleasant for those around you and most importantly, it is a bad example for adults to set for the younger Christians. I had tried many times throughout the years to quit without success. Now I reached out to Jesus in prayer and asked Him to help me. I asked Him to give me the desire to quit because there was a part of me that really didn't want to quit. I enjoyed smoking and it calmed my nerves when I had a cigarette. I told Jesus I was going to try it again and trusted that He would help me. This time I kept a pack of cigarettes with me at all times so that I could have one if the craving got too intense. I had never done this before. I'm sure the Lord put this idea in my mind to eliminate some of the anxiety. It worked. I just kept on going without a cigarette minute by minute, hour by hour, until, before I knew it, I had passed the crucial three month period. It was such a wonderful feeling to know that I was free from the ball and chain of needing cigarettes. I never realized how imprisoned I was by them until I was free.

When I had gone for two weeks without smoking, we had a visiting pastor come to our church from another state. At the end of the service he had an altar call for anyone who wanted to receive the baptism of the Holy Ghost. I knew what it meant. Just about all the churches we had been to since I came to Jesus believed in this, but somehow I had never asked to receive it. Now I knew it was time so I went forward. As they layed hands on me and began to pray I began to "speak with other tongues". In my case however, I just spoke one or two words and stopped. One of the ladies who was praying for me said, "Oh, don't stop or you'll lose it". I smiled and replied, "Oh no I won't". I knew the Holy Ghost was there to stay. Don't ask me how I knew, I just knew it! When the Holy Ghost came into my being, I felt the most gentle sensation in my chest that I had ever felt in my life, before or since. I knew that it was Him because nothing in me could be that gentle. This was very special because up to this point my impression or concept of God had been that of a mighty, powerful God. This is typical of our heavenly Father to totally do the opposite of what we expect He will do. I was bracing for a powerful sensation;

kind of a take over I guess, but Praise The Lord, that is not how He works. He does not take you over to the point that you no longer have control.

From this point on the Lord began to "open" the Scriptures for me. I began to understand them so much easier and quicker than ever before. Sometimes the Holy Ghost just gives a revelation of His word and ties Scriptures together for you.

John 14:26 says, "But the Comforter, which is the Holy Ghost, whom the Father will send in my name, He shall teach you all things, and bring all things to your remembrance, whatsoever I have said unto you". I was also filled with an overwhelming desire to know my God in a deeper more intimate way. This desire remains with me to this day and I pray it will never leave.

A few months after this we moved to one of our western states where my husband had another job in a band. We stayed there for two years and while there we attended a Baptist church and I was baptized in full immersion. After living here for a couple of years we moved to another state and while there, the church we were attending took a mission trip to Mexico and I went with them. They needed a base guitar player and so I went as part of the worship team. It was an awesome experience. We would set up in a local church and they would invite people to come to hear us play and the pastor would give a message. Somewhere in the middle of the service, our people would go into the middle of the people and pray for them. The worship team had to stay in place. Since I couldn't go out and pray for the people I stood and prayed quietly in tongues. I asked the Lord to let them see His love for them through me. It was absolutely incredible the love that I felt for those people. I knew it was from the Lord because it was not natural. At one point I looked up and saw a man standing at the edge of the altar with another person who was talking to him. When I looked into the man's face, I saw a look of total hatred. He looked like he would kill me if he could get his hands on me. It really scared me for a minute but I closed my eyes again and continued to pray in tongues. I repeated this about 4 times; looking up and then closing my eyes and praying. Each time I looked up I could see his expression softening. The last time I looked up, he was on his knees. He accepted Christ as Savior!

The night before we were to leave for home one of the elder ladies of our group came to me and said, "Bev, there is something I have to tell you. One night as I was in the church praying for people I asked the Lord to please let me see an angel. She said she knew there were angels all around and she wanted to see one of them. She said as she opened her eyes she looked directly up into my face and the expression on my face was just like an angel's." I can't tell you how much this blessed me because my prayer was that the people would see his love through me!

CHAPTER 5

MY HEALER

On Dec. 7, 1983 I underwent surgery for ovarian cancer. I had waited too long to seek medical help for abdominal pains which I had been experiencing for a few months. The cancer had grown to a mass about the size of a small football and it was attached to most of my intenal organs. The doctor who performed the surgery told me that I was very fortunate to have him as a surgeon because he was one of maybe three doctors in this country who would have bothered to operate on me. He said most doctors would have just sewn me back up and said "I'm sorry, there is nothing we can do for you".

What a "coincidence" that I would get him! No, I do not believe it was a coincidence at all. My Lord Jesus was in complete control. The Dr. had to cut the growth off everything and removed a small portion of the large intestine. When he told me the extent of the cancer after surgery, he said it was all through me including the lymph glands. (Years later I sent for a copy of my medical record and found that there were nodules on the liver, the pancreas and the duodenum. About 20 years later I shared the records with a specialist. He was amazed that I was still alive.) The first surgeon told me that they could probably keep me alive for a year with chemotherapy and radiation treatments. I was shocked! It is devastating to be told that you only have a year to live, if you're lucky.

To my husband's credit, he handled this like a trooper. He tried to keep me from hearing the worst of the diagnosis and was like a ministering angel as he watched over me in the hospital. I couldn't have asked for better care. As soon as I was able to go to the bathroom by myself I cried out to my Almighty God. I waited until then because it was the only place where I had any privacy. I was in a ward with several other patients. As I cried out to God I felt that I was before His throne. I really believed He heard me. I told Him that if this was His will and He was going to take me home, it was O.K. I was ready to go but I asked Him to consider the affect it would have on my Mom. Our Mother was a very special lady. She had eleven children and she loved each one of us with all her heart. I knew my death would be really difficult for her to deal with. Then I asked Him to please tell me if He was going to heal me. Many of my Christian friends had been telling me that the Lord had told them that I was going to be fine; but I needed to hear it from Him directly. This was much too serious to receive God's word second hand.

A few hours later I joined my husband in the waiting room. It was evening and there were only three of us there. I had my Bible with me and I chose one corner of the room for privacy. I opened my Bible and began praying: "Please Lord, speak to me through your word and tell me what you are going to do." I began turning the pages, just groups at a time. After just a few seconds I felt an impression to stop. When I stopped my eyes were drawn to one particular passage.

It was II Kings 20:5. It reads, "I am the LORD the God of your Father, David. I have heard your prayer, and I have seen your tears. Surely I will heal you."

My spirit leaped inside me! I knew it was from the Lord but immediately the enemy of our Soul spoke. "Are you crazy? Who do you think you are that the Almighty God would speak to you! You are letting your imagination run away with you!" So I did what I always do. I cried out to my Daddy God. "Father, I said. I believe that was from you and forgive me for asking but would you please confirm this word for me?" I left it at that. I didn't make any suggestions as to how He might confirm it. I left it up to him.

At this time I was in a hospital in NH. The church we had been attending out west knew of my situation. They sent me a Poinsettia plant to cheer me up. As

I picked up the card, I noticed a Scripture written at the top. It was "II Kings 20:5." The funny thing was that I didn't remember the scripture chapter and verse. I just remembered what it said--not where. I had to look it up to realize that it was the confirmation I had asked the Lord for. Tears of joy began flowing down my cheeks as I walked from my room down to the waiting room where my husband was. Honestly, to this day I'm not sure which made me the happiest. The fact that God Almighty, the Creator of heaven and earth and all that therein is, had actually spoken to me (This was the first time) or that He was going to heal me. I had not told anyone that God had given me this scripture; not even my husband so I knew it was the confirmation for which I had asked. Our Heavenly Father is so very kind and loving! He never fails to amaze me with the way He acts towards me.

I had about one week to rest before they were to begin the chemotherapy. One night my Pastor from church called. It was during their worship time before Bible study and he asked me if there was a special song I would like them to sing for me. I immediately thought of "Bless The Lord O My Soul" and when they sang it to me I could feel the presence of the Holy Ghost ministering peace and assurance in my heart and mind. During this time I kept praying; asking the Lord how He was going to heal me. If He would heal me through the medical treatments or just by Himself.

My friend (the one who made me a coat later on) had asked a certain Catholic lady who had the gift of healing to come visit me. She was a very special lady and I felt a connection with her right away. She also had a dynamic testimony. The Lord had healed her of Lupus "another incurable disease". She asked me if I would like her to pray for me and I said, "yes, please!" It was while she was praying for me that I had my first vision. She knew it was happening and asked what I was seeing. I told her what it was. It was a group of trees consisting of hardwoods and softwoods all mixed together which suddenly began to separate. At the end of the vision the trees were in two separate groups. She said, "I believe the Lord was telling you that He is beginning to separate His People from the world unto Himself." From the day that our Lord had spoken to me and confirmed His word, I felt very much at peace. This lady coming in and praying for me also helped to reassure me that I was going to be fine.

Then came the day when they would begin the chemotherapy. It was administered through an I.V. While they were preparing it I began praying; "Lord, if you don't want me to take this "chemo", cause it to mess up somehow." The Nurse put the IV in my arm and it began to flow down the tube but then something unusual happened. It wouldn't go into my arm! Three times she had to take it out, change it to the other arm and try again. The number three is a special number with the Lord. It usually is given as a definite sign. When it did finally work it went in so slowly that she even said, "I don't understand this. I've never experienced anything like this before. I can't imagine what is going on." I replied that I knew what was wrong. My system was rejecting it. But even then I didn't have the faith to tell them to stop. I told the Lord that if He was going to heal me without the "chemo" that He was going to have to do it without any help from me. I told Him that I knew I should have the faith, but I just didn't and I asked Him to please give me the faith to say, No to the chemo. You have to realize that chemotherapy was like a life line to me and yet I knew the Lord was telling me to let go. I continued with the treatments for the next few days. I had five bottles of "chemo" over a five day period. Half way through the treatments I became so full of faith that I knew it was not necessary for me to continue with them. I spoke with the Dr. about it but he said, "Bev, you only have a couple more bottles to go. Why not at least finish this set." It seemed like a reasonable request and I didn't think it made any difference to God so I said, "OK". By the time I was released from the hospital I knew that was the end of all treatments. I did not return to that hospital or any Dr. for at least one year. The gift of faith that my Father gave me was so deep and so strong that it didn't make any difference what anyone said, I just knew, that I knew, I would be fine.

When I left the hospital it was Dec.23, 1983. It was a very cold winter in northern NH that year. At first I went to my brother's home which was only about one hour ride from the hospital. While staying here, I had the privilege of praying for my brother for deliverance of alcoholism. He said he felt as if something had lifted from him as I prayed, but unfortunately, he still had a problem with alcohol. I stayed with him for two nights then we proceeded to my mother's home about 150 miles north of there. The heater in our car was barely functioning and the daytime high was about 10 below zero. I had a blanket wrapped around me but it was still pretty cold. The Dr. had warned my husband that if I caught a cold or any other sickness, he would have to immediately bring me back to the hospital because I had nothing in my immune system to fight it. Well, I did in fact catch a cold. Within a couple of days I was very sick. It was all I could manage to get up and go to the bathroom but I was determined that I was not going back to the hospital. One of my brothers said to me, "Bev, I know you believe that God is going to heal you, but you might have to go back in for a while." My reply was "No Sir! God said

He would heal me and God can't lie. If He can heal me of cancer He can certainly heal me of a common cold!" That was the end of that. Within two weeks my strength began to come back. I grew so strong so fast that I could hardly believe it. Everyone was amazed. Of course I did lose all my hair as a result of the chemotherapy. As I was recovering, the Catholic lady who had come to the hospital and prayed for me sent me a list of healing Scriptures printed in large letters on bright yellow paper. I hung them all over my bedroom so they were the last thing I saw at night and the first thing in the morning. She also had them typed out on regular paper so I could keep them with me. Whenever I felt a little sick or weak, I would read them out loud. It is much more effective to read out loud. They were my medicine. The enemy of my soul, the Devil, tried to rob me of my faith by planting doubts in my mind. Thoughts would come like, "are you crazy? Who do you think you are that God would heal you? You have cancer and it is all through you, you are going to die." As these thoughts would come I would command him to leave in Jesus name and continue to repeat that God had told me He would heal me and God can't lie. I would also stand in front of the mirror looking at my reflection and speak to the cancer. I would curse its roots in the name of Jesus and command it to die.

The "gift of faith" the Lord gave me got me through the first month then it gradually began to leave me. Reading the healing Scriptures fed my spirit and built a foundation of faith to replace the "gift of faith". I would continue to read these Scriptures for about six months until one day I felt the Lord wanted me to set them aside. I think I was beginning to put them in His place; almost as though they were becoming my God. I then would just cry out to Him if I felt pain or fear or doubt. I did the same as when I was in the hospital. I would pray and begin turning pages in my Bible. I kept going until I felt the impression to stop. Our Lord never once let me down. He always gave me the exact Scripture I needed. Sometimes it was a rebuke such as: "Am I a man that I should lie; have I not said it and will I not do it." Or, "cease striving and know that I am God". Other times it was just encouragement in telling me how much He loved me. This walk was new to me. It was not an easy path. I had to choose to believe the word the Lord had given me almost minute by minute for the first few months especially. As time went on it gradually became easier.

One year later while again visiting my Mom, I had a very bad virus/flu and had to see the Dr. for help. He asked if he could run some blood tests because of the cancer and I said, "sure." I was confident that there was no cancer left and I was right. There was no sign of cancer and has not been any sign of it since (33+yrs later). Years after this my oldest brother told me that because of this healing I received, he became a believer. This made it all worthwhile.

CHAPTER 6

MY SHIELD AND MY STRENGTH

Cancer patients are cautioned about living under too much stress while recovering, but that first year of recovery was very full of stress. The relationship between me and my husband was very tense. After the first few months of my recovery, we were in need of a place to live The Lord worked in the heart of a certain couple who were very good friends and they told us we could stay with them for a while. We stayed with them for about a month then another friend loaned my husband enough money to enable us to go back to one of our south-western states. My husband had been planning to do this since I left the hospital. As I write all of this down, it seems incredible but it actually happened. It was while living in that south-western state that the Lord would speak to me through His Word whenever I really needed to hear from Him, as stated previously. It was during this period that my faith grew greater as I had to rely on Jesus minute by minute.

While we were here I lost my beloved little dog which was devastating to me. I was heartbroken. The morning of the day he died the Lord warned me something bad was going to happen to him. As I knelt to give him his food, I was overwhelmed with the awareness that he was going to die. I won't go into details because it hurts too much still. He just never came home that night. (We let him run loose because it was country.) I should have handled things better than I did but I was not aware of how the Lord works at that time. When I received the warning, I should have kept him with us but I did not. I asked the Lord to watch over him while we went to the fireworks; it was the 4th of July. At first I was angry with the Lord because He didn't protect him, but eventually I would come to realize that the Lord did His part in warning me so strongly. It was then my responsibility to protect him. The Lord then comforted my heart and gave me strength to go on. After that we moved to another city for about two months. Then we moved back to TN for a short period. While living in TN the Lord led us to another great church. Sometime during this period I asked the Lord if He would allow me to feel the presence of the Holy Spirit inside me. I really needed to know He was there all the time. He answered my prayer almost immediately and I could feel a very gentle stirring in my abdomen, sort of like a miniature fountain bubbling. It was very comforting. At this time I was trying to acknowledge death as something I should not fear. After all, when we Christians die we go to Jesus so why should I be afraid of it

One night I had a dream where this big man came up to me at a party I was attending. The party took place in a huge basement. I had spotted him across the room and said, "Oh, there's my friend death". He then came over to me and put his arm around my shoulders and said, "Hi, Bev; how are you doing?" "I'm fine," I replied. Then I asked him if he was there to take me home. "No, it will not be for a while yet." he replied. Then he said, "the next time it will be in your breast." "Oh" I said. "Will it hurt much?" He replied," No, not much; only about like this;" and he pinched my arm. My reply was, "Well if that's as bad as it hurts, I guess I can stand it." My "friend" death then said he had to leave and he turned and walked away from me across the room. I noticed that he kind of waddled as he walked away, but I still could only see him from the head down to his waist. In order to leave the ballroom, however, he had to go up the large staircase. As he approached the staircase he turned to look back at me and he had a rather self-conscious silly smile on his face. Then as he progressed up the staircase his legs gradually came into view and I could see that they were terribly deformed. In fact they were twisted around each other. I was amazed that he managed to walk at all.

A few days later we went to our Pastor's home for Bible study. After the study I was with the ladies and told them of my dream. The pastor's wife said, "Oh no. Death is not your friend and that cancer is not coming back on you in any form." She then had me sit on a chair in the middle of the room and they all gathered around me and laid hands on me and prayed. They rebuked the devil and commanded him to stay out of my dreams then prayed for the Lord to protect me.

On the way home I asked the Lord why death's legs were so twisted. I knew there was some significance in this but I couldn't figure out what. I then felt the Holy Spirit bubbling stronger than usual inside me. It was like a bowl of jello bouncing around in my tummy. I knew He was laughing and so I asked Him what was so funny. As clear as could be I heard Him say, "he didn't have much to stand on did he." I joined him in laughter at that point. I was laughing so hard, my husband who was driving the car, asked what I was laughing at. When I shared with him he laughed also.

After a few months I asked the Lord to please make the bubbling inside me to stop. I told Him that I did not want to offend or hurt His feelings, but the sensation was beginning to bother me because it was not a normal part of my being. It immediately stopped and I have never felt it again. I do feel that if I ever really wanted it back, He would return it.

CHAPTER 7

GOD's FAVOR UPON HIS CHILDREN

Psalm 5:12 "For thou, LORD, wilt bless the righteous. With favor wilt thou compass him as with a shield."

During one of our stays in the south-west we had a special restaurant that we would go to when we could afford it. Some German people had recently bought it and the food was delicious. Sometimes we would buy one plate and share it if we couldn't afford two dinners. On one of these occasions when the waiter brought our meal he had a separate plate for me; my favorite. I protested that we had only ordered one meal and he said, "Oh, it's O.K. This is from them", and pointed to a door which was slightly open into the kitchen. His parents were peaking out with big smiles on their faces. Tears filled my eyes and I had to fight to gain control as I managed to say, "thank you". I believe this was just one more way the Lord showed me his love. Also during one of these stays in this state it became necessary for me to find another place to stay for a while. I called our Pastor and explained my situation. She told me to pack up some clothes and she would come pick me up. The first night I stayed with her and her husband. Normally I would have been very upset about my circumstances, but somehow I was not. I was very calm and sure that everything was going to be O.K.

In the middle of the night I woke up laughing. I had pulled the covers up over my head and I was curled up into a ball in the middle of the bed. I actually woke myself up because I was laughing so hard. I hoped that my Pastor and her husband couldn't hear me for fear that they would think I had lost my mind. It was the Holy Spirit who was making me laugh but He didn't tell me what He said or did after I awoke. I'm sure there will be a time when He will tell me what He did. All I knew then was that I felt great! I was not the least bit depressed or worried about what was going to happen to me.

The next day the Pastor took me to one of her daughter's home. It turned out that she and her husband were separated. I stayed with her for a couple of weeks. I took care of her two children while she worked and helped with the housework. The Lord also used me to help her and her husband reconcile. While there I asked the Lord if He would help me to get back to NH. One day a lady from our church came over and said to me, "Bev, I don't know what your plans are but the Lord told me to give you this money." I don't remember the exact amount but it was over $100. But then circumstances changed again and I was able to return to my home. I believe that if I had checked the bus lines, the money she gave me would have covered my expenses to get back to NH.

Not long after this we returned to NH and we again stayed with the same friends that had taken us in before. We were with them for a couple of months when Peter managed to get enough money together to head back down to TN. He wanted me to go with him but this time I refused. I just couldn't bring myself to go through all that again. He was gone for about a month then came back to NH. While he was gone I stayed with my Mom, but when he returned we went back and stayed with those same friends. After a few months our welcome was wearing thin. It became obvious that our presence was causing problems between our friends and I just couldn't let that happen. I had been praying for a place for us to live but as usual we had a very limited income. One day the lady of the house talked with her brother who was currently living in CA. He had a house that was empty close to where we were staying. She asked him if he would consider letting us stay at his house and he was happy to do so. Rent free! He also was a Christian and a very good friend. It was an old house which had been renovated but still was heated by a wood stove only. They had had an electric or gas stove but that was gone so the only stove to cook on was the wood stove which I really didn't mind. Unfortunately, the water pipes had frozen during the winter and although it was now the middle of March, they were still frozen. I really didn't care. I was thrilled to have a place where we could be by ourselves and not impose on anyone. Our friend's mother lived just across the driveway in a small house and we were able to get water from her. While we lived here for the first month or so my husband was very good about getting in the wood and getting up early to make sure the house was warm by the time I got up to prepare for work until he began working in VT.

I had been praying all these years to change me or my husband to make us more compatible. Finally, I told the Lord that I would not leave my husband because I knew he didn't like divorce, but I did ask if it was all right with him to please make my husband leave. I didn't care how he did it, short of taking his life.

I had managed to get a job at an insurance agency which paid quite well. I was also selling Tupperware. As tension increased between me and my husband I had to quit the Insurance job. My nerves couldn't handle any more. Please don't misunderstand me. I'm not saying everything was my husband's fault. We just simply did not mesh.

One night as I attended a Camp Meeting, a minister whom I had only seen a few times, came up to me and gave me a word from the Lord. He said, "The Lord wants you to know He loves you very much and He wants you to know that he has heard your prayer and He is working. It won't be too much longer." I had not told anyone that I had asked the Lord to take my husband out of my life. This word was a tremendous encouragement to me.

I finally moved in with my Mom because winter was approaching and I didn't want to stay in that house by myself. I did leave enough of our things there so that we could return if necessary. The following January, 1986 was the last time I saw my husband. He came for a visit and left me the best of our two cars for which I was very grateful. Marriage problems are rarely one sided and I am no more perfect than anyone else. We just did not work together.

CHAPTER 8

Jesus now began to reveal himself as my Comforter. Even though it was a relief to not have to live with all that tension, I still felt the rejection. One day I was walking on the country road that ran past my Mother's home which I did on a daily basis. I was talking to the Lord and thanking Him for the peace I felt and for the beauty all around me. It was fall and one of those legendary New England days with crisp air, bright blue sky and magnificent fall foliage. As I was thanking the Lord and praising Him for his goodness and for the beauty of this world he created, my thoughts turned into poetry. I love poetry but it isn't a common occurrence for my thoughts to just flow in rhyme. I knew it was the Holy Ghost and I laughed out loud, thanked Him for doing this, and just let it flow. What a wonderful experience! Our wonderful, merciful and loving Lord had me enveloped in his presence. Awesome! His peace, reassurance and love just filled me to overflowing and I was sure all was well.

During this time my friends (the Associate Pastor who had married us and his wife) offered me a room in their home where I could go whenever I felt the need to be alone. I was always welcome there and I deeply appreciated their hospitality, friendship, counsel and spiritual wisdom. This was another tremendous blessing for me.

CHAPTER 9

MY LEADER AND TEACHER

Shortly after returning home I attended our little local church. On this particular Sunday our Pastor had a friend visiting who was also Spirit filled and functioned in several gifts of the Holy Spirit. It was a Communion Sunday and we all went to the front to receive Communion. When she came to me she paused for a moment and then said: "While you were sitting in the pew I saw the Holy Spirit hovering over you and I watched as He poured out his anointing oil upon you". This will sound ridiculous but I didn't know what "anointing" meant. I went home and told my Mom what she said. She didn't really know what it meant either. I began searching my Bible and came to the understanding that it meant God had given me the Spiritual ability to accomplish whatever he calls me to do.

This was not the first time I had received a "Word of knowledge or prophecy" from someone. While attending the christian women's meetings and some of the women's retreats, I was sometimes told I had a special "call" on my life.

I now turned my whole focus on the Lord. Since the Lord had healed me of cancer many of my fellow Christians felt that the Lord must have something special for me to do. I began praying for direction. I felt so inadequate for the Lord to use so I decided I had better go to Bible College and get some training and education. Please note that I said, "I decided". This decision was determined more from logic than the Lord's guidance. I decided on one particular college and my decision was really based on the fact that it was the least expensive of all. I attended this Bible College for one year. At this time I was 41 years old.

The school was located in a southern state and I drove my old car down all by myself. It was a Buick; I don't remember the year but it was at least ten years old (70's). Just a simple car without any extras. It did have air conditioning, which was a blessing. With the Lord's help, I made it safe and sound.

On the first day when all the students were assembled for a special service the president spoke a message which he said was from the Lord and I believe it was. I felt that he was speaking it to me. The message was as follows: "Thou hast felt like Hagar - one placed without the camp. Yet in the wilderness have I not given thee cool water to drink and daughter; saith the Lord, thou art called of me. My hand is upon thee. The enemy has sought to sift and the enemy, at times, has even deceived and has led thee this way and that way; but, my daughter, this night, saith the Lord, if even afresh you will put your trust in me, I will not lead thee deep in the wilderness, but I will lead thee home. Yea, I will lead thee out, saith the Lord. I will lead thee out of the things that have sought to hurt and to harm and to wound thee; out of confusion, out of despair. I, the Lord, who hast fed thee, clothed thee and cared for thee, shall lead thee, saith the Lord your God."

While here I also had a dream one night in which the Lord spoke through the president of the college's mouth and told me that he had planted me in my own land. I knew without a doubt that it was the Lord's voice. This dream was very real and the Lord's voice was tremendously powerful. I believe this meant that He had a particular work for me to do.

Attending this school was a good experience because I learned that the Lord is able to guide me and protect me through anything. I would find out later that the leaders of the school were not walking as Christians are supposed to walk. I could see that there were problems but I felt that I needed to keep my commitment to finish out the year. I had a bad habit of starting something and then getting bored with it and quitting. I felt that the Lord wanted me to finish the one year and so I did. There were some good people there whom I really loved and sincerely hope that they are now doing well. While I was there, I worked as Secretary to the President of the school. This was against my will, but he insisted. The Lord did use my circumstances there to show me that He is always with me and is able to watch over me and protect me anywhere.

At one point during the year, they were going to ask me to take on another responsibility. I cried out to the Lord because I did not have any more time available. The Lord took care of the problem. Just before I was to begin my new task, the need was taken care of. I also called on the Holy Spirit to help me retain all the information needed to pass each course. He was faithful to help and I was able to pass each one as one of the top students. There was one course that I was not able to attend very often because of my work schedule and I did get an "incomplete" in that subject.

About halfway through the year one of my nephews was killed in an auto accident. When I got the call from my brother, Ira, I almost lost it. All of my family are very special to me and to lose one while I was so far away and unable to go home was twice as traumatic. Somehow, the Lord calmed my flesh and comforted my heart through His Spirit. I also was comforted and encouraged by some very special people at school. God is good! I was also comforted in knowing that my nephew was a Child of our Lord and I will see him again in heaven.

As the year came to an end, I told them that I was going home for the summer. At this point that truly was my intention. I was asked to reconsider and stay at the school during the summer so I prayed and asked the Lord what he wanted me to do. Three times within one hour He gave me the Scriptures of Mark 5:34, Mark 5:19, Luke 8:39 and Luke 8:48 which all basically say "return to your people and tell them what great things the Lord has done for you, and go in peace". After this I felt sure that it was O.K. for me to leave. As the time of my scheduled departure approached, the President and the Dean brought more and more material for me to type for them. I was not the only secretary in the school but you sure would have thought so if you had seen the work piling up on my desk. They did not want me to leave because many students who left for the summer did not come back. I could understand why.

The day before I had planned to leave I received another call from my brother, Ira. He and his family had been vacationing in Florida and were on their way home. He said they thought they would stop in to see me because it was right on their path home. I was so happy to hear that because I had been having some problems with the radiator in my car. A local mechanic had plugged a few holes but he said I really needed a new radiator. It was a little scary facing that long drive home by myself, but now I would be able to travel with my brother and his family. It was a great comfort and I knew the Lord had worked this out for me. I worked on the morning of that last day, typing as fast as I could. When my brother arrived I asked them to please put all my things in my car. (I had not had time to do so.) He and his wife did as I asked and I typed all morning until my brother said they had to be going. I left a note for the teacher that I was typing for and departed.

That night as I visited with my brother and his wife in their motel room, I suddenly realized that I felt as though I had just escaped from prison. I spent a lot of time praying before finally making a decision to not return to that school. By the way, my old Buick got me home with no problems. Praise be to our Lord and Savior!

Joel 2:28 "And it shall come to pass afterward, that I will pour out my spirit upon all flesh; and your sons and your daughters shall prophesy, your old men shall dream dreams, your young men shall see visions; vs.29 And also upon the servants and upon the handmaids in those days will I pour out my spirit."

After I returned from bible school I was asked to consider the position of Lay Leader at my church. I did accept the position and during this time we had a group of young ladies from southern NH come to visit/minister. They gave testimonies of how the Lord had delivered them from drugs and alcohol. I decided to fast for the group before they arrived. After two days of fasting when I awoke in the morning as I began to get out of bed I closed my eyes for a second and as I did a picture appeared. Surprised, I opened my eyes and the picture immediately disappeared. So I closed my eyes again and the picture reappeared. It was a huge container (like a barrel) above my head. Then it slowly tipped over and something began to pour out over me. I opened my eyes and said, "Lord, I believe this is a vision and if it is from you, would you please bring whatever is pouring out up closer so I can see what it is." I closed my eyes again and immediately I saw beautiful golden kernels of wheat within a foot from my eyes. I was so excited that I had had another vision and this one was perfectly clear. I told my Mother about it as we ate our breakfast then I realized that I didn't know what it meant. After praying for a few minutes and asking the Lord about it, the word "bounty" came to me loud and clear. The word came from within but not from my mind. The Lord then led me to Scriptures that speak of the Lord dealing bountifully with us (Psalm 116:7) and of the finest of the wheat (Psalm.147:14) There are several other Scriptures as well that speak of these same things. In all of these experiences the Lord was revealing Himself not only as the great "I AM" but as my loving and patient Father.

In Hebrews 11:6 it says, "He is a rewarder of them that diligently seek Him".

I was definitely seeking Him and He was rewarding me.

There were a couple of other blessings from Him also. There are some big, fat flying bugs that come out in the month of June and are called, "June bugs". They don't bite or do any harm but if they land on you, they kind of stick. Anyway they are rather offensive and we avoid them as much as possible. Like most bugs, they are attracted to light. My Mother liked to stay up late and read. This was her habit for as long as I can remember. One night I noticed that a lot of these June bugs along with other kinds had accumulated in the window. In this particular Mobil Home the screens were built into the inside of the window and there were outside windows that opened with a crank. The bugs were between the outside window and the screen because she had the outside window open to let in fresh air. In order to clean out the bugs it was necessary to go outside and brush them out. This was not my favorite job to put it mildly! I remarked to Mum that

I would have to clean out the window in the morning and asked her to remind me. She knew how much I hated the job and said that she would do it. Mum had emphysema and was in the advanced stages of the disease. It was all she could do to walk from one end of the mobil home to the other never mind go outside and clean the window. I told her it was O.K. that I would do it.

As I proceeded to prepare for bed, I remembered the Scripture about God being a husband to the widows. Technically I was not a widow, but I was without a husband so I talked to God about it. I said, "Father, your word says that you are a husband to the widows and a father to the orphans. Well, right now I do not have a husband and my father has been with you for a long time. I have no man to help me. If my husband or father were here, I would ask them to clean out that window for me and they would. Lord you know how much I hate that job and I would really appreciate it if you would clean that window for me before morning." I wasn't sure if He would do it or not but I didn't have anything to lose in asking. The next morning the window was totally and beautifully clean!

My mother thought I had done it when she got up and was quite taken back when I told her I didn't. She was visibly shaken about the incident until I told her about my conversation with my Lord. Even then, she didn't quite know what to think about it. As for me, I was delighted! Why does it seem wrong to ask our Father to help us with physical tasks. First Corinthians 12:10 where the gifts of the Spirit are listed, mentions "the working of miracles" as one of the gifts. He is a Living God and He likes us to "acknowledge Him in all our ways".

My clothesline also got repaired without us being aware of anyone fixing it. It was one of those clotheslines with a center pole seated in concrete. The pole had gotten bent over so much that I couldn't use it. One day when I got home from work I looked out at the clothesline and it was fixed. My mother didn't know anything about it. I asked around but no one would admit to fixing it. Even if one of my family or neighbors did fix it, they were sent by my Lord.

One day I was resting on the couch and closed my eyes for a moment. All of a sudden I could see this beautiful country spread out before me and then I was flying over it. I was not in a plane; I was simply flying. The land was quite hilly and all the grass was cropped short as if someone had mowed it. There were no trees in sight. As I looked at the size of this country and all the mowed grass, I remarked to the Lord that this couldn't be real because no one would mow all that grass! Then as the vision continued I came to a place where I could see trees on the sides and then mountains. The mountains had quite pointed peaks, like volcanoes, and the far side of them gradually sloped down into the sea. There were no clifts. Then I came around over some falls where the vegetation looked like something you would see in a jungle. Then on to a bay area where there was a small village. While in this place I felt that there was another piece of land off in the distance, although I couldn't see it. A few years later after I had married my current husband, I told him about this vision and he remarked that it sounded like New Zealand which he had recently visited. He had a couple of books with pictures of New Zealand and some of the pictures were exactly as I had seen in my vision.

Shortly after I had this vision, I was told that it must be a place that the Lord was planning to send me as an evangelist. This upset me because for the first time in years I was home and no one was pressuring me to go somewhere else. I love New Hampshire and most of my family were there. I did not want to leave. So, one afternoon as I was driving home from work, I asked the Lord; "Why do you require people to leave their homes and family? Is it to prove their love for You? You know our hearts and you know whether we love You or not and how much. So why do we have to leave our loved ones? I'll go if that's what You really want but I'd rather not have to." Sometime later on I opened to Scripture which reads; "because I have loved you, I have sent someone else in your place." I felt that he was saying, "It's O.K., you don't have to go and I have never had the opportunity to go to New Zealand. That doesn't mean I never will, however.

CHAPTER 10

ANOTHER MIRACLE

During all this time I was involved with the Christian women's group. I even had the opportunity to speak at a few meetings and was the main speaker at one particular meeting. I spoke on growing up in Christ and it went quite well although nothing special occurred. It was the custom of this group to hold a special banquet once a year and members could invite husbands or other men. It was at one of these meetings where my niece introduced me to a certain man who later became my current husband. I had not been seeking another husband at all nor had he been seeking a new wife. We were sure it was the Lord's hand that brought us together and two months after we met we got married.

This began a whole new phase of my life. Seven months after we were married my Mom died. We knew it was coming but it was still very difficult to deal with. I missed her terribly and without realizing it, I sank into a depression. Then about one and a half years after we were married my husband was diagnosed with a malignant brain tumor. When the Dr. told us he had a brain tumor which he was quite sure was malignant, I think I just said, "Oh Lord" very quietly. I had a very dear sister-in-law (the wife of Ira) die of a brain tumor a couple of years prior to this so I knew what to expect. I remember thinking, O.K. Lord just give me the strength to cope. A very dear friend was with us and he also responded very quietly. The Dr. asked me and our friend to please step out into the hallway so he could examine my husband privately. When we left the room the Dr. remarked to my husband that he did not understand our reaction, or lack thereof. He told my husband that people usually scream or run up and down the halls when he tells them such bad news. My husband replied that our calmness was because of our faith. He asked where do you get faith? My huband told him JESUS: that we simply trusted JESUS to take care of the problem one way or the other. Out in the hallway reality hit me and I did cry for a few minutes. Our friend asked me if I had had any idea that this was coming and I told him No, but we just had to trust the Lord and take it one day at a time. The Dr. who made the original diagnosis came to northern NH from Yale-New Haven Hospital. This Dr. transferred Greg to Dartmouth-Hitchcock Memorial Hospital in Lebanon, NH. The same hospital where

I had surgery for the ovarian cancer, except that this was a totally new $750 million hospital and Greg was the first neurosurgery patient. The one I had been in was so old it had been torn down and replaced with a new building in the nearby town. (Greg says, that "God had this hospital built just for him.") The surgeon who performed the surgery on my husband was also sure it was a malignant brain tumor prior to surgery. On the morning of his surgery, I was alone in the waiting room praying for Greg and wishing someone could have come to be with me. Then I looked up and saw a couple walking towards the waiting room. It was Ira, whose wife had died of brain tumors, and his new wife. He was absolutely the last one I would have expected to come. He told me that the Lord had spoken to him that morning and said he wanted him to go and be with me. When he told his wife, Louise, she never argued or questioned what he said. She just said, "O.K., Let's go." The Lord blessed him with a real sweetheart for his second wife as well as his first. This brother is also one of the Pastors at their church. We were all praying, of course, and my husband told me later that he had told the Lord that if he was going to be a vegetable for the rest of his life, that he did not want to wake up from surgery. Our Lord performed another miracle because the "malignant tumor" turned out to be an abscess. It was a very strange abscess because when they put a sample of it in a dish to let the bacteria grow so that they would know what medication to administer to keep it from growing back, no bacteria grew. Ten days after surgery my husband came home from the hospital. He never had a seizure of any kind nor any need for physical therapy. His recovery was miraculous. (Had it been an abcess he would have died before we got him to the hospital!) The Dr. who had diagnosed the tumor initially began calling my husband at home and questioning him about our faith. He gradually came to accept Jesus as his Savior. Salvation is the greatest miracle of all!

CHAPTER 11

THE LORD AS MY HEALER
(AGAIN) AND MY PROVIDER

I was fighting a mental battle during all this time without realizing what was happening to me. Through prayer, I began to pull out of the depression but I was also dealing with confusion and memory loss which continued for another five or six years. After I had surgery for the cancer, I entered into menopause. This was a couple of years before I met my husband but at that time it was not bad enough to recognize it as a real problem. I had also been having anxiety attacks but I didn't know what they were. Sometimes I would feel that I could not deal with life or any of the simplest of tasks before me. When this happened I would cry out to Jesus and He would get me through. Peace would come over me and I would just go on.

In the meantime, my husband was without employment. He had gone through a divorce a couple of years before we met and in the process, lost his job which was a very well-paying position. He has a PhD in Chemistry. You would think he would have found a new position quickly but it did not happen. We even traveled out west as far as Utah and he did have several interviews. Each time the potential employer would cause us to believe that my husband had the job but then we would not hear from them again. We returned to NH when my Mom died and stayed in her Mobil Home which was now owned by my brother, Raymond, who also is one of the Pastors at their church. We remained here for three long years. This was a tremendous time of trials and testing and growing in faith. It was during this time that my husband had brain surgery, which made it even more difficult for him to find employment. Our finances were slim and none. I managed to get a part time position which barely paid our utilities. I remember driving home from work thinking, "Well Lord, I have no idea what we will have for supper because my cupboards are pretty bare, but you have promised that we will not go hungry." When we got home we would find a bag full of groceries sitting on the porch. Sometimes we knew who left them, but most of the time we did not. One time we found a Cashier's check in the mail box with no return address on the envelope. These were special Christian friends who did not want any thanks or gratitude. They were just doing what they knew the

Lord would have them do. My husband's dear Father also helped us out during this time. He would call and ask if we needed some money and my husband would always tell him no, we're doing O.K. Within a week from his call we would receive a substantial check from him. He was also a good Christian man.

During all this time the Lord kept telling us, to "wait on Him". Also, "I have done it, and no one can deliver you out of my hand". One day while visiting friends, the wife handed my husband an ad for employment that she thought he might like to answer. My husband took it home and it sat on our kitchen table for three weeks before he finally said, "well, I guess I might as well try it." He really didn't think he was what they were looking for but what did he have to lose? It turned out to be the answer to many prayers. He did get the job and the Lord provided a rental car for us. (We no longer had a vehicle of our own. We had been borrowing an old car from my brother Raymond). Interestingly, the day before my husband left for the interview, Raymond came over and told him that the Lord had told him that he would get the job but there was something he would have to bargain for. That something was the rental car!

CHAPTER 12

THE LORD, MY DELIVERER

We then moved to central NH while my husband worked in northern MA. Life was so much better now except that I was having more severe mental problems. Things had progressed to the point where I was seriously considering telling my husband to put me in a nursing home and forget me. Just doing my housework was a major task. Sometimes it was too much to deal with and so I would get in my car and go for a drive on the country roads around our town. This did calm me down and I would enjoy the countryside and pick up fresh vegetables at roadside stands. When I finally realized how bad I really was, I prayed with all my heart and asked the Lord to help me. I told Him I could not go on like that. One day I was alone in our apartment watching a Christian program and the host of the program had a "Word of knowledge" concerning a woman who had a tormenting spirit hovering over her. He began to intercede in prayer and suddenly I felt a "pop" above my head and the voice I had been hearing (which I thought were my own thoughts) was gone. One of the problems I had been having was that whenever I thought to do something, even housework, I would hear this "voice" saying, "Why do you even try, you know you can't do anything right. Why don't you just run away. Nobody loves you or wants you around anyway." On and on it would go condemning and discouraging me. From the day that host prayed, the voice was gone. Needless to say, that was a tremendous help and it was the beginning of my healing of the mental problems.

We rented the top floor of an old Victorian mansion which Greg's boss had purchased. The home had been many things over the years including a nursing home. It turned out that there were several "familiar spirits" sharing the top floor with us. One day I realized that when I stood near the large radiator in the living room, I could hear deep even breathing, like a person in a deep sleep. My husband and our daughter also noticed it. She asked me if I realized that we had a radiator that breathed. I just laughed it off but was really kind of concerned. Our daughter had also seen a man in the basement dressed in a fancy sport coat of the 1800's which had instantly disappeared. Then one night at 2 AM the smoke detector in the attic started beeping. We couldn't get to it without a ladder, so we had to wake our landlord to help. By the time he and his wife got upstairs, all the smoke detectors on our floor were beeping at various intervals. It was like musical chairs played with smoke detectors. As we would stand under one, it would go silent then one in another room would beep. I had told them that I thought there was a spirit up there that we needed to cast out but I don't think they believed me. They were good strong Christians also, in fact we went to the same church, but this was a little too much I guess. As we stood in the living room listening to the musical smoke detectors, with no sign of smoke or unusual amount of heat around, our landlords finally took me seriously. "What can we do?" they asked. I told the husband that because he was the head of the house, he was the one who should actually do the speaking. He said, "O.K. what do I say?" I told him to speak to any and all evil spirits that were in this house and tell them to leave this house and his property and to not return in Jesus name. We stood in a circle and joined hands as he prayed and we all agreed with him in Jesus name. When he finished speaking, the beeping had stopped and we never had a problem with them again. Also, we did not hear the radiator breathing again nor did the gentlemen in the basement ever reappear.

CHAPTER 13

WORKER OF MIRACLES

Each morning my husband, Greg, would leave for work at 6:30a.m. and from the time he left until around 9:00a.m. I spent my time with the Lord. I would read for awhile then put on some of my Christian tapes and sing and dance in my living room unto the Lord. Then I would pray for specific things and just spend time talking to Him. One morning after everyone had left except for one other boarder who rented a studio apartment on the second floor, I could smell burnt toast and plastic. I caught him just as he was leaving and asked him about it and he agreed that he smelled the same thing. He checked the ground floor when he went down and said everything seemed to be O.K. It is not unusual for someone to burn toast and the smell of plastic in our house was not unusual either. There was a plastic company of some sort just a mile down the street. As time went by however, I began to see a very light film of smoke in my apartment. I went downstairs and could smell it stronger down there but there was no sign of smoke coming under the doors and I couldn't see any sign of fire anywhere. I went back upstairs where I was again watching the Christian program and I prayed to Jesus about my concern. I opened all my windows and doors so the smoke would go out, thinking that if someone had burned their toast it would take a while for the smoke to reach our apartment. I also specifically prayed, "Lord Jesus, if there is a fire in this house I ask that you put it out. Send some angels to take care of it or just take the oxygen out of it and smother it." I also said that I would leave the windows open for a few minutes but if the smoke continued then I would call the Fire Department. I really didn't want to do this unless I was sure there was a fire because I know they have to break down doors to get in and if there was a fire they would really ruin everything with water, etc.

Our landlord had just renovated the two first floors which was a lot of work and expense for them. After I prayed, the host of the program spoke into the camera and said, "There is a lady out there who was in a potentially very dangerous situation, but you are all right. Whatever it was, the Lord has taken care of it." I really felt that he was talking to me. After a few minutes the smokey haze disappeared from our apartment and the smell grew fainter.

When the landlord got home he discovered there had been a fire in their kitchen. Their toaster handle would not snap up after the toast was done. They had to lift it up manually. It seemed that the last one to use it had forgotten to lift up the handle. The toaster burned down into the antique table it was sitting on and also burned a large hole in the side of another antique cabinet sitting beside it. Inside of the cabinet were several empty milk bottles which had all melted down. He called the Fire Chief to come and make sure that there was nothing that could rekindle. The Chief was totally amazed that the fire had gone out. He said he would never have believed anyone if they told him something like that had happened. In fact he said, "I'm seeing it with my own eyes and I still can't believe it. There is no way that fire could have just gone out. It was as if something sucked all the oxygen out of it and smothered it!" Our Lord is an awesome Lord!

During this time as I spent so much time worshiping the Lord, reading His Word, and praying in the Spirit, I had several beautiful experiences with him. As time passed, I grew increasingly hungry for a deeper relationship with the Lord. I knew it was possible but somehow I just couldn't press through. One morning I cried out to Jesus. "Lord", I said; "I know it's possible to have a deeper relationship with you but somehow I can't get through this wall between us. Will you please help me." As I spoke these words I was sitting on the edge of our couch. This began a "spiritual experience" like none other! I closed my eyes and saw Jesus hanging on the cross directly in front of me. The next thing I knew I was there with Him. His chest was a mass of raw flesh covered with His blood. At first I felt repulsed by all the blood and tried to pull away but I was held securely by an invisible force (The Holy Spirit). There were just little pieces of flesh left on His chest. There was one piece near my right hand and I felt an awful urge to pull it. Almost simultaneously to the urge I felt ashamed and guilty for feeling so. Then the Lord spoke to me and in a voice incredibly gentle and full of love He said, "go ahead, Bev; take that flesh and peel it off - as much as you want." I felt confused and embarrassed, I really didn't understand what was taking place but I did what He said. At first I felt a little guilty or reluctant but He encouraged me to do this. He wanted me to hurt Him. He wanted me to know that this was why He died on the cross. This was all part of His suffering. A lifetime of pain and hurts and rejections in me were transferred to Him as I tore that piece of flesh. He gladly, willingly and totally encouraged me to do this. He bore my hurts and all the pain and humiliation of my whole life. As I did this and obeyed Him, He revealed to me that I had been a part of His suffering. I was ONE for whom HE DIED ON THE CROSS! This was always His plan for mankind. I was amazed at the reality of the experience. I could feel the reality of the "Man" Jesus' His flesh and most especially, His blood! It was flowing all around and over me then through me. It was so comforting and healing and it washed my soul. I was aware of the tremendous strength in His body.

When His ministering to me had finished, I rested on His chest for a few moments declaring my total love for Him and knowing for the first time that I totally belong to the Lord Jesus. I am in Him and He is in me! I asked Him to forgive me, which He lovingly did. Then I felt so bad because I had added to His tremendous pain by pulling away His flesh, which tore deep into His chest near His heart. I said, "Oh, my Jesus, I'm so sorry I hurt you too." and then I tried to put the flesh back, somehow trying to minister to Him. Instantly I was aware that this was a wrong thing for me to do. I had to give Him my pain in order to become His. That's what He is all about. I had resented the fact that our "Loving and Merciful God" had allowed pain and hurt in my life. He certainly could have prevented those experiences and I couldn't understand how He allows His children to be hurt and then dies on the Cross because He loves us. I knew it was painful for Him; but He is God. It didn't prevent my pain; and that is still true. I never realized that He really can take away the effects of painful memories. When I admitted that I had a problem with this and realized that because of this problem I had not opened my heart completely to the Lord, I asked Him to help me. When I told Him I wanted to open all my heart to Him but I just couldn't and asked Him to help me if He could; I was willing to let Him help me, that is when this experience began. I need to tell you that this was a very real experience. He took me there and allowed me; excuse me, He caused me to hurt Him as much as I felt that I had been hurt. He loves me that much! And you too.

This was a totally beautiful, loving "HOLY" experience. Everything that happened was HOLY for He is Holy. When it was over I knew that He had made me holy. His love, His blood, His actions made me holy. I was totally pure and clean. White as snow! God is so Good! Amen! After I had rested on His chest for a few minutes, I suddenly became aware that it was over and He began to fade and pull away, up into heaven. The cross and He were no longer visible but were like vapor which was full of light and power. This mass kept rising up into heaven then kind of settled, and tremendous "clouds" of light and power in the colors of deep purple and blue began to emerge billowing and rolling up and out. I could feel or sense His majesty and awesome strength. As the clouds came towards me, a small portion came to my face and seemed to flow through me, entering in through my eyes and nose. I stood still and felt strengthened and refreshed. Instantly it was gone and I became aware that I was sitting on a rock and at my feet was a brook. It was an arid spot, desert like. I asked the Lord, "where am I, what is this place?" The name "Kidron" came instantly into my mind. This has significance. The Kidron brook borders south-eastern Jerusalem. It is the place where they took the idols of false gods and smashed them into powder and poured the powder into the brook. I felt the Lord was saying that I now had entered in to a greater relationship with Him.

The next day was March 8th and it was the 4th anniversary of my Mom's death. It was a very peaceful, restful day. I felt that the Lord was respecting my feelings and giving me a day to just relax and remember her. She was a very special Mom and I still missed her very much.

On Mar. 9, 1995, I lifted my hands to worship the Lord and almost immediately I felt the Holy Spirit come into me in great power. It came in waves, as if He filled me to the brim, waited for it to settle then poured in some more. It continued for a few minutes. I felt so much power inside I was sure I could do anything the Lord might require of me at that moment. It was absolutely awesome!

When this had finished, the Lord began to speak to me. "This day have I birthed a new thing in you". Then He paused and very emphatically said, "Go, get paper and pen and write this down." I obeyed and He began to speak as fast as I could write; in fact I began to write in shorthand thinking I could do that faster, but He impressed upon me the feeling that I didn't have to worry, He would not go faster than I could write. He continued, "A new work will I do through you. You are my own, my chosen special child. In you I will reveal the love I have for all my children - my Church - my Bride. You will be my messenger. You will speak as I command and nothing else! I AM The Lord!" There was a slight pause, in which I rested as I praised Him with all my heart! Then He continued; "You have been in the furnace of affliction but I was with you as with Shadrach, Meshach and Abednego. Now are you refined - by MY fire. I have done it! You are MINE! You have been purchased by My blood and I have sealed you by My Spirit. WE ARE ONE!" The last two sentences were spoken with such emphasis that I knew He absolutely meant that I belonged to Him totally! I was no longer my own person. I am sorry to say that my flesh rebelled against that knowledge. After all, the essence of our sin nature is to be our own God. We want to be in control, not to be controlled by God. The wonderful thing about our Lord though is that He doesn't force or overpower us. He gently leads and loves and encourages us to do His will. After this Jesus led me to various Scriptures in Isaiah confirming how He planned to use me. He also led me to special events I had made note of in my old Bible and some of my journal entries I had made in the past few years. Some of these were confirmations to the fact that I had received a "very powerful anointing from the Lord"; others were special times with the Lord. At last He led me to find notes that my Mother had written. Some were about the Lord and one was just a part of the poem, "Barefoot Boy", which was one of her favorites. I could almost hear her saying, "from my heart, I wish you all the joy in the world my dear daughter". It was so very special! I knew it was the Lord's doing.

CHAPTER 14

Not long after this we were introduced to a lady who had a counseling ministry. She had helped many people who had emotional problems and marriage problems. I called her and asked if she would be willing to counsel me. She agreed to do so and for about one year I would meet with her once a month while she led me through a series of healing ministries. One of them was titled "The Refiner's Fire". (Another one of those "coincidences") She was also a Spirit-filled Christian and the Holy Spirit worked miracles through her in emotional healing which in turn helped heal my mind. I also discovered that too much caffeine could cause confusion and as I talked to my Dr. about my problem, he checked my thyroid gland and found that it was not working properly. Slowly my mind got better; back to normal. Praise the Lord Jesus!

About one week after the experience on the cross, I had another spiritual encounter with our heavenly Father. I was again crying out to the Lord as "Abba

Father " (Daddy God). Suddenly, in my mind, I was a little child; three to four years old. My Daddy God was holding me in His lap. He was sitting on his throne, with His crown on His head. When I realized that this was a real Spiritual experience, I submitted to it and let my feelings go. This was an on-going emotional healing process continued from the one on the cross.

Now I was seeing my Lord as the resurrected KING! He was in all His majesty. His closest guards were all around near Hs bed chamber and throne. I was in His "private chamber". At first I was only aware of being on His lap. He let me play with His crown for a few minutes then I lovingly and gently put it back on His head where it belonged. A little crooked which He straightened. His attitude towards me was of total love and patience. I was free to be myself. To do anything my little heart desired. I was playing as a child would play. I could see myself as a child with my long blond hair curled into ringlets. I was totally free and very happy. He was allowing me to just be me. He didn't speak and neither did I; except to keep calling Him "Daddy God" and to tell Him I loved Him to which He would reply, "and I love you, my dear, precioul little child. I love you very, very much." It was a very special time. I was expressing my love and at the same time experiencing the presence and love of my Father. I would put my little hands on both sides of His face and look deep into His eyes and see His steady, unflinching gaze of pure love in return. All the time He was healing me although at the time, I was unaware of it. I didn't realize this until later as I remembered the experience. Sometimes I would relax and lean against His chest, feeling the warmth, the strength, protection and love. I was just drinking in His reality and His personality. These are things a child will do with their father. In fact I used to do this with my earthly father who died when I was ten years old. I was even aware of the Lord's physical smell, which was very masculine. Sometimes I would stroke His beard, then I would get down and run around the room to the window and back; just being a child but also to be sure He was still there. I would climb back on His lap whenever I wanted to and He would take me up and hug me and always let me do whatever I wanted to do. I had a real sense of being free to be myself and that there was no hurry. He was giving me all the time I wanted or needed. I had His undivided attention. He was all mine! He also made it clear that He was not to be interrupted!

Afterwards I realized that His guards were given to understand how important I was and am to the Lord. Gradually I began to grow up; even as I sat on His lap and walked about the room. My appearance began to change from a small child to a teenager to a young woman. Constantly surrounded and protected by my Father and His guard. They would smile at me and let me know they would protect me totally. This they did without speaking; somehow I was made to know this. At some point the Lord was with me at the window, as if He was showing me His kingdom and letting me know that as His child, I am heir to all that is His. His royal guard is there to serve and protect me. They will surround me and go before me. I will always be under protection by my Father's orders! I also am to be allowed entry into His private chamber at any time. He will always be there for me! Praise His Holy Name! All of these experiences, spiritual and physical (the healing ministry with my Christian sister and the medical treatment for thyroid) brought about my healed mind.

During the next five years the Lord was my constant helper and companion, healer, friend and Father. Whenever I had to attend an event concerning my husband's company, I would always ask the Lord to show me what to wear. I would simply go through the clothes in my closet, touching each piece I thought might apply. When I felt peace come over me as I touched a particular garment then I knew it was the one. This never failed me. He also helped me to select new clothes at the stores in the same way.

One time I was planning to attend a special women's conference and I needed a small weekend piece of luggage. I really didn't want to go buy one because the conference itself was quite expensive. I felt the Lord impressing me to be patient; that He would supply one. Usually when the Lord does something it comes at the last minute. This exercises your faith and patience. Greg had gone to Atlanta on a business trip and arrived home two days before I was to leave for the conference. Guess what he had with him. Right! A small piece of luggage which had been a gift from the meeting he attended. It was just perfect--even the color which was black & purple. This may seem trivial to some, but it was these little episodes that blessed my heart in a very special way. It was Jesus way of saying, "See, I love you so much I will take care of all that concerns you." I needed His help in these things. It took a lot of pressure away.

CHAPTER 15

My oldest brother lived in Connecticut. He told us his niece (on his wife's side of the family) was just diagnosed with cancer. He asked if I would call her because he thought that talking to someone who had been through it might make her feel better. He said it appeared that the cancer had gone into her lymph glands. I did call her and she was so grateful for my call. It seems that I was the only one she had talked to that had been involved with this type of cancer that had anything positive to say. After talking with her, I felt the Holy Spirit was drawing me to go visit her. I decided I would speak to Greg and if he agreed, I would know the Lord was in it. As it turned out, Greg suggested we go visit her before I asked. As I sat in her living room next to her on the couch, the Holy Spirit suddenly took over. It was amazing. I had been wondering how I would know what to say or what to do when all of a sudden I just began to speak of the fact that I was living proof of the healing power of God. For at least two hours the

Holy Spirit used me to witness, teach and encourage her. I believe He healed her at this time. Greg was very supportive. A couple of times I felt I should stop and as I did, the Lord would speak through Greg. It was an amazing, wonderful experience. She did have surgery to remove a tumor but there was no more sign of cancer. Praise the Lord!

CHAPTER 16

The Lord again reveals himself as our provider. My husband began to have severe Migraine headaches along with some other physical problems; one shoulder in which he had torn the rotator cuff and one hip which had hurt him for a long time, caused him almost constant pain. Then one day he called me from work and said something was wrong. His mind wasn't working right. He couldn't speak at times. The Dr. said he had probably had a small stroke. After this he applied for temporary disability from work and was approved. About six months later it was apparent that he would not be able to return to work. He was able to collect from an insurance plan and disability from Social Security. These were both a blessing from the Lord.

We made a down payment on a cottage on a pond back in northern NH. While living here, the Lord continued to bless us. We had to put a new carpet in the living room which was a sizeable room. My husband had to rip up the old one and was really not up to the task. My friend, the Pastor from my previous marriage, came and helped Greg take it out. The cottage also needed to be painted and we began to do the job ourselves. It was a very slow process for us as we attempted to do it with brushes. I asked the Lord to please help us as it took us one day to do just a 6' x 6' section. Greg was only able to work for about an hour at a time before having to rest and might not feel like working again for quite awhile. It was cedar shakes, which never should have been painted in the first place but someone had painted them so now we had to do the same. The next day a friend came by and told us that he had a sprayer which would be a lot quicker. He came by shortly thereafter and as he proceeded to show us how to do it he ended up finishing 3/4 of the house in one day! The other friend, who had helped with the carpet, came and finished the job later on. He had to use a scaffold to finish it. Greg never could have done this. We were so very thankful to our Lord for sending friends and taking a monumental task out of our hands! Every time something came up that was difficult for us to handle ourselves, the Lord sent someone to take care of it for us. What and awesome God we serve!

CHAPTER 17

New Hampshire has a lot of Moose and my husband always wanted to shoot one. You have to apply for a special permit in order to do this. They then draw names to see who gets to hunt them and which location. He applied and a few days later asked me to put my name in also so that he would have a better chance to win a permit. I did as he asked. It turned out that we both won a permit and in the same section which was in the next town. This was very exceptional! The Lord was with us both. Greg shot his moose just as the season opened. Almost in the first five minutes! It was also the largest female shot in NH that year. The Lord Jesus was so good to him because he knew that Greg would not be able to stay out hunting very long. I got my moose, a smaller male, which was actually the best meat, the next day. We were allowed to take one extra person each with us on the hunt. We chose two of my nephews to accompany us. The nephew with me shot my moose because he came out right in front of him. I was glad he did because I wasn't sure I could actually shoot one. I probably would have, but I was glad I didn't have to do it. One of these nephews was also in the logging business and had a skidder to get the moose out of the woods on to the road and a friend hauled them to the weigh station with his truck. The Lord Jesus made it all as easy as possible. We ate moose for a long time! It is really quite good. Our heavenly Father is so wonderful! Praise your name, Jesus!

The cottage we were living in was heated by a combination furnace that used either wood or fuel. We used wood most of the time because it was less expensive. This also was quite difficult for my husband to do. After a couple of years my Aunt's home became available as she went in the Nursing Home. My brother Raymond and his wife Diane now owned it and we asked if we could rent it from them. They agreed and so we proceeded to sell the cottage. We bought a small "For Sale" sign at Walmart and nailed it on to the front lower corner of our cottage. That's all we did. Within a month we had two people inquire to buy it. They came on the same day. We got the price we wanted without dealing with a realtor. Again, our Father provided so easily.

CHAPTER 18

In the fall of 2005, I dreamed of Kentucky three times in a row. I knew my husband's family were originally from Kentucky but this was the first time I had dreamed of it. I told Greg about it and said that maybe we should go there for the Winter. Greg had continued to deal with almost constant pain. He barely did anything except lie on the couch. Winter was worse because the short days and extremely cold weather made him depressed. He did manage to go for a walk most mornings. There was a small dam nearby and we would walk around the canal which amounted to a couple of miles. It was a beautiful spot and we enjoyed it greatly but we didn't go very often in the winter. We decided that it would be nice to get away and so we closed up our home and off we went.

To make a long story short, we ended up in TN through one of my husband's cousins. We had a house of our own to stay in and only had to pay for the utilities for the first couple of months, then the landlady added a small rent charge. We made a deal with the owner to watch her two Golden Retriever dogs while she went on trips for a week or sometimes three weeks at a time.

It wasn't long after living in TN before I knew that the Lord wanted us to move here. It was just an impression that wouldn't go away. It also became very obvious that Greg felt better here. I'm not sure why; maybe the lower altitude but he definitely felt better. He was also diagnosed with Sleep Apnea while we were here. As he began to feel better, we became more engaged in things we used to do like hiking or just taking a day trip now and again. We actually began to live a normal life!

As the winter drew to an end we began making plans to go back to NH and prepare a move to TN. Although I knew the Lord wanted us to move to TN my heart just wasn't in it. All of my family are in NH and that is where I wanted to stay. My thought had been to just spend winters in TN, not to move here and I began to plead with the Lord to work in a different way. Finally, I relented. I told the Lord that I would go and that I would set my mind to love TN; to be happy there and not feel sorry for myself. As soon as I did this the Lord began to bless me. He blessed me with help in getting things packed and in finding a niece who needed the furniture we had decided to leave behind. She and her husband came and picked it up just before we left.

We were at that time living in a mobil home. It was a nice mobil home with a couple of rooms added on and a two car garage with lots of storage room in the back. However, we were told that we would not be able to get the price we were asking because the banks would not give a mortgage on a mobil home no matter how nice it was. We replied that if the Lord wanted it to be sold for our asking price, it would sell. We were right. One afternoon we were outside working on the garage when a couple came by. They said that they had heard we might be leaving and wanted to know if the house was for sale. We told them our price and we had to come down a little, but still within our range. Again, we did not have to involve a realtor. This time we didn't even put out a "for sale" sign!

We rented a large U-Haul van to move our things. We had two vehicles; a car and a medium-sized pick-up truck. The plan was to put the car in the van with the furnishings, then one could drive the truck and one the van. I was going to drive the van! My husband was not well enough to drive it; in fact, I was concerned about him driving the pick-up truck. Believe me, I was not looking forward to driving that big van. I kept telling myself, "I can do all things through Christ who strengtheneth me". Philipians 4:13

At the same time I was praying that He would provide someone to help. About two weeks before we were due to leave, Greg's cousin from TN called and said he and his wife had decided that he should fly up to NH and drive the van back for us! I can't tell you what a relief that was! Just one more blessing from my Daddy God! Praise His Holy Name!! As we settled in to our new home in TN, (which is perfect for us) the LORD actually made my statement a reality. I do love it here and I am very happy. Our home is in the country at the end of a lane on a river. I like my privacy and this fits the bill perfectly! Praise you Lord Jesus!

CHAPTER 19

I mentioned previously of dreams that I have had where the LORD spoke to me. Many of them were personal messages. This one in particular was a message that I believe the Lord wants me to share. In this dream I was with two other women who also had been healed by the Lord. We were at a huge convention center where we had been called to give our testimonies. There was a stage at one end of the hall and as I waited backstage for my turn. I felt the presence of the Lord. The Holy Spirit stirred in my heart and I began to sob; heart-wrenching sobs that shook my whole body. I knew the Lord was upset and was about to speak through me to these people. I didn't know what He would say but I knew He was angry; very hurt and displeased with them. I did not want to go out on that stage but I knew I had to for the Lord. I walked out on the stage and I said, "I have something to say to you from the Lord. You are not going to like what I have to say but I must speak it. It is from the Lord." I opened my mouth and these words came out. "I am the Lord Jehovah. The great and Holy God of Israel. I am the God who created the heavens and the earth. I am the God who created you, who formed you from the dust of the earth and breathed life into you. It is not a big thing that I heal you and yet you question my ability to do this. Even those of you who do believe for a while soon turn back to your old ways of skepticism and unbelief. I am the God who brought my people out of Egypt. I split the sea and they walked through on dry land. It was not through shallow waters as you have been told. I caused the river to run red with blood and the water in the fountains and water pots to be turned into blood; It was NOT red clay as you have been told. I the LORD did all these things and yet you do not believe that I am a living God! You limit me, the Holy One of Israel. You make graven images and pray to them yet I am not in them! (There were several statues of various Saints around the hall and as I spoke these last words, each one of them EXPLODED into dust!). Absolute chaos broke out as people screamed and began running in sheer panic. However, some remained in their seats. The Lord continued speaking; "Turn your hearts and your eyes unto me for as I have said,

"If my people who are called by my name shall humble themselves and pray, and seek my face, and turn from their wicked ways then shall I hear from heaven and I will forgive their sins and I will heal their land". (II Chronicles 7:14)

Yet you will not listen. You continue to walk in unbelief! At this point my alarm went off and I awoke.

The Lord says in His Scripture in Numbers 23:19 "God is not a man that He should lie, nor the son of man that He should repent: hath He said, and shall He not do it? Or hath He spoken, and shall He not make it good?"

Through all of this, I felt the LORD'S compassion and His anger. He loves us so very much and it hurts Him so greatly because we don't believe the Words of His BOOK and because we listen to men explain away the Scriptures. These men sometimes lead us astray because we don't take the time to ask the Lord if what we are being told is His truth. We must always bring these teachings to the Lord and trust Him to acknowledge His Truth. He is a living God and He will answer us.

CHAPTER 20

One year after moving to TN we received a phone call from our daughter, Alysia who lives in NH. It was one of those calls that you pray you will never receive. She had been diagnosed with breast cancer! Greg is one of those rare people who does not panic in emergency situations. He very calmly told her that he was sure she was NOT going to die and to just take it one day at a time. He said, "do what the Dr. tells you and trust Jesus to get you through this." I have to say that it was easier for me to trust the Lord for my own healing then it was to trust Him for Alysia's healing. Don't ask me why, it just was. Praise the LORD, this was not so for Greg. He did want to be near his daughter, of course, so we packed up in the middle of winter and went back to NH.

We were blessed in that some of our dear friends took us in to their home and treated us just like family for three weeks. Normally we would have stayed with my brother Raymond and his wife, Diane, but circumstances did not allow this at that particular time. After three weeks we were able to go and stay for another week with Raymond and Diane. During all this time we spent as much time as possible with our daughter going with her for treatments, taking her out to dinner or visiting with her at her home. The time came when we felt it necessary to return home. We continued to pray for her and as Greg predicted: she came through it all O.K.! She only required minor surgery! Thank you my Holy Father!

Shorty after this emergency passed, we received another emergency call from Alysia. This time she was about to undergo surgery on one eye. The retina was detached and the Dr. was not sure he could get it perfectly back in place. She asked Greg to pray for her which he immediately did. Again, he reassured her that she would be O.K. When he hung up the phone, we prayed together seeking our Lord and His healing power with all our hearts. The surgery was successful! The surgeon was able to get it perfectly in place and, as far as I know, she has no problem with it at all. A few years later she told us there were questionable cancer cells in another part of her body. We continued to pray and we praise our Lord Jesus that it turned out not to be cancer.

CHAPTER 21

The latest healing I received from the Lord was of Vasovagil Syncope which is very bad fainting spells accompanied by dizziness, vomiting and diarrhea. This particular disease is often fatal according to our Dr. and he said, "it was good that Greg does not panic or you might have died during an episode." People do not get healed of this malady. The last spell I had was in Oct, 2010. When I fainted I fell face first. My nose was bleeding and I had cut my lip. My husband cleaned my face and the floor of all the blood before I regained consciousness. As I was coming out of the faint, I could feel two sets of hands caressing my face and the back of my head. I could also feel love so strong it was almost tangible. I could feel it all through me and I felt wonderful. Then I heard my husband calling me and suddenly felt nauseated again. I knew I was regaining consciousness but I didn't want to leave those hands and the wonderful love that I was experiencing. However, I did have to leave them and as I regained consciousness, Greg asked me where all the blood was coming from. I put my hand to my lips and my nose and looked at them. There was no sign of blood. I asked him what blood he was talking about. I believe I actually died during that episode and the LORD HEALED me of the Vasovagil Syncope. I was sure I died because the bleeding had totally stopped. I did not have any clots in my nose and I could feel and see the cut on the inside of my bottom lip. Also, it was the greatest love I have ever experienced. Again, I thank my Lord Jesus and Praise His holy name!

FINAL THOUGHTS

The LORD continues to bless us as He works in us, through us and around us. Life goes on with the "tribulation, Jesus said, we would have in this world," (John 16:33) but as they come so also do the blessings. The LORD continues to bless us as He works in us, through us and around us.

There are other dreams that I have had which I did not include in this book. I have also had other special times where the LORD has spoken to me. Sometimes He speaks to me through His Word and other times I hear His voice which comes from within my mind. Other times He just causes me to know something as in the case with my dog.

I have no idea what the Lord has in store for me in the future and it really doesn't matter as long as He continues to speak to me and let me enjoy His presence in my life. Through all of these years and experiences with my Lord, I have learned to trust Him regardless of what is going on around me. Nothing is too difficult for Him to handle and nothing is too small for Him to care about. It has been through some of the smallest blessings where He has shown His greatest love for me.

The absolutely greatest expression of His love, of course, was His sacrificial death on the cross for all of us. I pray that this book gives absolute glory and honor to my Lord Jesus Christ. I also pray that all who read it will be blessed in some special way but especially that if anyone reads it who does not know the LORD, I pray they will come to know Him by the time they finish reading it. I do know that the LORD has not blessed me with so many miracles and blessings because I am some extra special person or of super spirituality. I am neither of these.

Years ago my sister-in-law, Marie, gave me a wall plaque with Matthew 5:16 on it which reads, "Let your light so shine before men, that they may see your good works, and glorify your Father which is in heaven." This Scripture raised a question in my mind. If they are my good works, how does that glorify God? The answer is, we can do NOTHING on our own.

In John 15:5 Jesus said, "I am the vine, ye are the branches: He that abideth in me, and I in him, the same bringeth forth much fruit: for without me ye can do nothing."

Therefore I rest in the fact that any good works I do are in fact done by my Lord Jesus, not only for my benefit but for all who "see" them. I praise you my great Lord and King, Jesus Christ and thank you with all my heart! Amen!

John 3:16 says, "For God so loved the world that He gave His only begotten Son, that whosoever believeth in Him should not perish, but have everlasting life".

Philippians 2: 5 -8 says, "Let this mind be in you, which was also in Christ Jesus: Who, (being in the form of God), thought it not robbery to be equal with God; But made Himself of no reputation, and took upon Him the form of a servant, and was made in the likeness of men: And being found in fashion as a man, He humbled Himself, and became obedient unto death, even the death of the cross".

Three days after this He was resurrected and appeared to His disciples and gave them instructions for their new life. (John 20: 19-31) His death on the cross atoned for all the sins of mankind. His resurrection brings us into reconcilliation (literally to be one with) with the Father and eternal life. The only requirement is, as stated above in John 3:16, you must BELIEVE IN HIM. I hope you will make this choice today and then find someone and tell them of your choice and find a good Bible believing church. This will help you to form a good relationwhip with the Lord and to keep growing in your knowledge of Him. May our Lord Jesus bless you in your new life. Amen.

Beverly D. Kennard

ACKNOWLEDGMENTS

I would like to thank my friend, Perry Hartman, for his efforts on this book and his prayer support. My husband, Greg, deserves the greatest thanks for his patience, editing, and prayer support.